TULUM

Text
Archeologist Luis A. Martos

Cover
The Castle and The Caribbean Sea

Half title
Polychrome ceremonial vessel,
Dzibanché, Quintana Roo

Photographs
G. Dagli Orti
Archivo Monclem

CONACULTA · INAH
Reproducción autorizada por el
Instituto Nacional de Antropología e Historia

Translated by: David Casteldine

© 2006, Monclem Ediciones S.A. de C.V.
Leibnitz 31, colonia Anzures 11590
México, D.F.
www.monclem.com
e-mail: monclem@monclem.com
Tels.: 55 45 07 39 • 52 55 42 48

Printed in Mexico
Impreso en México
ISBN 970-9019-39-2

Contents

The Maya culture

▶ The Mayas were real masters at bas-relief work in stone, as shown by this image from lintel 26 of Yaxchilán, Chiapas. In this representation, the ruler B'alam II can be recognized, who is receiving the head of a jaguar from his wife, a symbol of power and hierarchy.

The Mayas occupied a vast region that includes the present-day Mexican states of Campeche, Yucatán and Quintana Roo, areas of Tabasco and Chiapas, and also Belize, parts of Guatemala and Honduras and western El Salvador.

In antiquity, the Mayas were divided into ethnic groups with similar physical characteristics, though with some local features. Similarly, they spoke languages belonging to the same stock and shared one and the same historical and cultural tradition, also with local variants.

According to experts, 4,500 years before our era, a proto-Maya group settled in the Chucumatanes Heights in the present Department of Huehuetenango, Guatemala: in the course of time, this ethnic group broke up and gave rise to the different languages of Maya affiliation and their later migration resulted in the formation of the extensive Maya territory. This in general terms, is subdivided into three major areas; the Highlands of the South, which consist of the mountainous regions of Chiapas and Guatemala; the Central Maya Area, comprising the Department of El Petén in Guatemala and the outer adjacent valleys of the Northern Lowlands, which are on the Yucatán peninsula. Each of these major areas is in turn subdivided into regions, based on geographical and cultural criteria.

The early migrations of proto-Maya groups led to the establishment of contacts with other civilizations from which the Mayas adopted cultural forms. Some authors assert that the origin of Maya development must be sought in the Guatemalan mountains where corn seems to have been domesticated: from there it later spread to the north and west, although the influence of other cultures is probable, including the Olmec.

To this effect, other specialists think rather that it was in the lands in the north of Tabasco and the south of Veracruz where contact with the Olmecs must have been closer. This culture developed mainly in the lowlands of Tabasco and Veracruz between the years 1300 and 600 B.C. and it has been considered a sort of "Mother Culture" since they created many religious concepts, stylizations and symbolisms that other great Mesoamerican cultures adopted and developed later. From the Olmecs, the Mayas appear to have

▼ Most Maya buildings were profusely decorated with colorful murals of masterful concept and workmanship. In this scene, a procession of lords presents captives on the staircase of the acropolis after being taken prisoner in a battle. Bonampak, Chiapas.

taken the beginnings of an ancient mathematical and calendar system in addition to some symbolical and religious ideas.

Although from 550 B.C. a Maya physiognomy takes shape, it was not until 250-300 A.D. that it showed its own personality clearly, free of all earlier influence. Between the years 300 and 600 A.D., a period known as the Early Classic, numerous Maya cities arose and developed with a complex system of social, economic and political organization. Nevertheless, the greatest height was reached in the Late Classic (600-900 A.D.) when cultural and scientific expressions reached their peak and most of the cities flourished: Palenque, Comalcalco, Yaxchilán Toniná, Edzná, Becán, Calakmul, Tikal, Caracol, Uaxactún and Copán.

After this period, during the Late Classic (800-900 A,D,), the so-called "Maya collapse" happened, a phenomenon recognizable by a serious sociopolitical crisis that culminated in the abandoning of nearly all Maya cities.

The cause of the Maya collapse is still not known with certainty, but a combination of factors has been surmised, like a prolonged drought, soil exhaustion, expansion of the bureaucratic machinery, social and political conflicts, as well as attacks by foreign groups.

What is certain is that the classic Maya world came to an end and not only did all construction of buildings, erection of stelae and production and exchange of polychrome pottery cease, but nearly all the cities were abandoned; only in the north of Yucatán did contact with groups from central Mexico revitalize the culture to a certain extent and enable the great centers to survive 100 years more.

From the 10th century until the year 1200, Maya tradition fused with the Toltec from the High Plateau. The Itzáes, who identified with it, established their capital in Chichén Itzá, a city that acquired features similar to those of Tula, although enriched by Maya sensibility and plastic art.

Chichén Itzá did not fall until the year 1250 and the Cocom inherited supremacy in Yucatán; there they exercised from their capital of Mayapán a cen-

◀ Figurine from the island of Jaina, Campeche. It is a portrait of a Maya hierarch with all his attributes. This site is famous precisely for the great number of tombs discovered with the magnificent offerings of vessels and pottery figurines.

tralized government that ended with attacks by the Tutul Xiu around 1441.

After this period, Yucatán was organized politically into at least 16 different chiefdoms. This division is what the Spanish found at the time of the conquest in the 16th century. The Mayas were characterized by the development of a particular style expressed in architecture, sculpture, stucco modeling, mural painting and polychrome pottery, areas in which the subjects and the workmanship show great uniformity; similarly, the development and use of complex calendar and writing systems are fields characteristic of this people.

The Mayas built great urban centers with monumental architecture: tall pyramid temples, palaces, ball courts, "acropolises," dwelling-administrative-ceremonial complexes with buildings and patios standing on bases and platforms on different levels.

An outstanding feature of the architecture is the use of the "false arch" or "Maya vault," which was used to roof the rooms, precincts and entrances to the buildings and in the structures known as "arches", or votive monuments erected just at the beginning of some *sacbé* or white roads. The latter served to connect the different architectural groups of a city and in turn this with other urban centers.

Around the ceremonial centers stretched extensive dwelling areas inhabited by the common people, who lived in huts of wood or palm.

Another important Mayan feature is the inclusion of sculpture in architecture, which can be seen on the facades, roof crests and bodies of the pyramids.

The social structure of the Mayas was pyramid-shaped, headed by the *Halach Uinic* (True Man), sovereign and lord, representative of a hereditary dynasty. Below him were the nobles, priests, warriors, merchants and artisans; on the lowest level were the peasants.

CHRONOLOGICAL TABLE

YEARS	PERIOD	CITIES	CHARACTERISTICS
2500 B.C	LOWER PRE-CLASSIC	PROTOMAYA	• Division into Huastecos and Mayas • First ceramics
1200 B.C. 400 B.C.	MIDDLE PRE-CLASSIC		• Population increase • First cities
200 A.D.	UPPER PRE-CLASSIC	DZIBILCHALTÚN / KAMINALJUYÚ / CALAKMUL	• More complex ceremonial centers • Clear social division • Beginning of polychrome ceramics
600 A.D	EARLY CLASSIC	TIKAL / CALAKMUL / PALENQUE / BONAMPAK	• Beginning of the dynasties. Splendor of the Classic period
800 A.D	LATE CLASSIC	RIO BEC / TIKAL / PALENQUE / BONAMPAK / PUUC	• Consolidation of dynasties • Beginning and development of major wars
900 A.D.	END CLASSIC	PUUC	• Important contacts with groups from Central Mexico
1250 A.D	EARLY POST-CLASSIC	CHICHÉN ITZÁ / TULUM	• Power of Chichén Itzá • Fall of Uxmal
1521 A.D.	LATE POST-CLASSIC	MAYAPÁN MANÍ / TULUM	• Mayapán, last great domain of centralized power

9

To feed the large population centers, the Mayas developed a type of subsistence based on intensive farming, with the use of terrace systems in hilly areas, raised fields on low-lying land and irrigation systems that made use of rivers and lakes and the channeling of rainwater. The main farm products were corn, chile, squash, cotton and cacao. In addition, around the houses there were orchards of fruit and medicinal trees. Hunting and bird raising provided meat, and the production of honey and wax was very important, especially in Yucatán.

Local and regional trade was essential to the Maya economy: different objects were exchanged: pottery, textiles, jade, shell, flint, obsidian, skins, precious feathers and other products.

One of the most important achievements of Maya culture was the development of a complex system of hieroglyphic writing, which appears at least from the year 250 B.C. and was considered a sacred means of communication.

Maya inscriptions, which can be counted in thousands, were carved on stone, on stelae, lintels, tablets, staircases and stucco reliefs or were drawn in mural paintings and even on pottery.

Maya writing was "logosyllabic," in other words, the different signs were equivalent to syllabic sounds and also to ideas or particular actions. The subjects dealt with in inscriptions are especially historical or religious and tell of the life and activities of the nobility, the deeds of the lords and gods, the alliances, marriages to join lineages, the births of future lords, the deaths of important personalities, lists of rulers of a dynasty, the ascent of a new king, wars, the building and consecration of temples, the performance of certain ceremonies, etc.

The system of numerals was vigesimal and was based on the position of the values and the use of zero, which was represented by a design in the form of a conch shell. The dot was used to signify units and the bar had the value of five. In addition, there were 20 ideograms for the numbers zero to 19.

The Mayas also invented a calendar system consisting of a sacred calendar or *tzolkin* of 260 days and a civil one of 365 days or *haab* made up of 18 months of 20 days plus five ill-omened days known as *uayeb*. In addition, they were able to plot the movements of the sun and the moon, the

▲ The "Blue House" at Calice in Quintana Roo, is a good example of the polychrome look which the temples of the east coast must have displayed, a region where the archaeological site of Tulum is located. In this mural, painted around 1450 A.D., the colors blue, gray and ocher predominate.

cycles of the planet Venus, and eclipses with great accuracy.

Maya religion had some concepts of unity that brought it near to monotheism, although in other aspects it was polytheistic. The creator god and main deity of the ruling dynasties was *Itzamná*, who had an infinite number of avocations; the god of Rain was *Chaac*, the chief god of the Maya peasants. The god of corn was *Yum Kaax* represented as a bearded man. The sun god had several names, including *Ah Kin*, *Kinich Ahau* or *Kinich Kakmo*. The goddess of the Moon was *Ix Chel*, who had an oracle on the island of Cozumel and was also the patroness of medicine and births; other notable gods were *Ek Chuah*, the god of trade and *Xaman Ek*, the god of the North Star, since he was the guide during trading journeys. Other important gods were *Ah Puch*, the god of death, and *Buluc Chabtan*, the lord who oversaw human sacrifices and was also patron of war. Towards the 10th century, due to contact with groups from central Mexico, *Kukulkán* – the feathered serpent – was incorporated into the vast Maya pantheon, and worship of him acquired great importance, especially at Chichén Itzá.

Tulum through time

▶ Lithograph by Frederick Catherwood showing the aspect of the Castle during the visit the famous artist made in 1842 in the company of the explorer John Lloyd Stephens. The picture shows the impeccable state of conservation of the building and the look of the site completely covered by jungle.

When the Spanish arrived, the east coast of Quintana Roo possessed a great cultural complexity, as well as an intricate social, political and economic structure, developed over the course of many centuries.

The east, or Mexican Caribbean coast consists of the coastal fringe of the state of Quintana Roo, which stretches for more than 900 kilometers from Cabo Catoche on the northeast side of the Yucatán peninsula to the channel of Bacalar Chico on the border with Belize.

Although the Mayas occupied these coasts at a late date, they developed a culture with its very own characteristics and strong personality from the 1st century B.C. until the Spanish conquest. Without a doubt, Tulum is the most representative and important site on this spectacular coast.

It stands 127 kilometers south of Cancún and 47 kilometers southeast of Cobá and is located on a prominent cliff facing the Caribbean Sea; it is a splendid city encircled by a defense wall on three of its sides, since the fourth is well guarded by the coast itself. The site arose and grew vigorously between the XII and XVI centuries in the period known as the Late Post-Classic.

One of the most notable features of the region is the so-called "east coast architecture,"

a style distinguishable by its excessive generalization and uniformity. It includes buildings that tend towards horizontality with few decorative variations, and is based especially on the use of a combination of moldings which outline a frieze, either plain or with some kind of decoration.

Originally, Tulum was part of a complex settlement together with another site called Tankah (a little earlier than Tulum). This complex was known earlier as Zamá-Xamanzamá and seems to have been a political unit, perhaps the largest on the coast. In appearance, Tulum is a Post-Classic extension of the occupation of Tankah, which began activity in the Upper Pre-Classic, around 150 B.C. In fact, Tulum appears to be a renaissance of the community of Tankah, with the need to erect a new and imposing ceremonial center placed on a more favorable and protected site.

The location of Tulum on the cliffs, with the addition of the walls, made it an extremely inaccessible site, with the advantage of having a small beach that made communica-

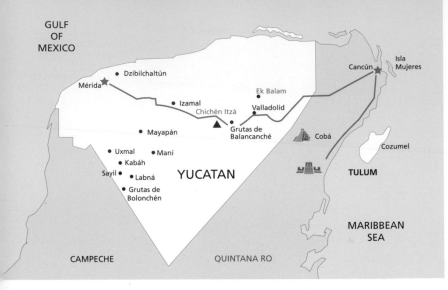

tion by sea possible; in addition, the adjacent beaches to the south were convenient places for embarking and disembarking canoes.

Like other Maya cities, the inhabitants of Tulum were divided into three well-differentiated social strata: a dominant class represented by the dynasties of rulers and the nobility, responsible for the affairs of government, religion, war and long-distance trade; an intermediate class devoted to the production of artifacts, local trade and personal service of the dominant class, and an inferior class subject to service, farming, fishing and hunting.

The highest social classes were those that lived inside the walled precinct, an area that no doubt was the civic, administrative and ceremonial sector, where the palaces and temples stood. It appears that religion had an essential function in Tulum society, as attested by the numerous temples, shrines and altars, some still with remains of stucco molding and mural painting, with particular allusions to rain, fertility and life, in addition to representations of the worship of the Descending God, the divinity also venerated in other coastal cities such as Ichpatuun, near Chetumal, and also inland, for example at Cobá.

The real identity of this god is not known for certain; some authors relate him to the evening sun and others with Venus, rain and lightning, a swallow god worshiped on Cozumel and even with a bee god called *Ah Mucen Cab*.

Tulum means "fortification, trench or city wall," a name it was given in recent times due to the wall that surrounds the site, although its original name was Zamá, a word that appears to be a corruption of Zamal, morning or dawn.

The first mention of the site is owed to Juan Díaz, chaplain of the fleet of Juan de Grijalva, on May 7, 1518. The next reference to Tulum dates from 1575 and is included in the Account of Zamá by Juan Darreygosa, guardian of the "encomendero" Juan Martín.

Again Zamá is mentioned in the Catalogue of Churches (1582), but seems to have remained almost deserted shortly afterward and in 1668, the Indians of Polé (Xcaret) were gathered in the towns of Bolonia and Chemax, located inland.

After this, there are no known records of Tulum until 1840, when Juan Pío Pérez noted that Juan José Gálvez had visited the coast of Ascension and stated that between this port and El Cabo there were two ancient cities: Tacná and Tulum, the latter surrounded by walls. Later, in 1842, the famous voyager and explorer, John Lloyd Stephens, accompanied by the artist Frederick Catherwood, visited the site and brought it to the world's notice in the book about their visit published in 1843.

During the War of the Castes in Yucatán (1847-1928), Tulum was occupied by Maya rebels and became an important shrine for the cult of the "Talking Cross." In fact, an important Mayan Indian priestess called María Uicab lived there, who was known as the "holy patroness" or "queen of Tulum."

During this time, visiting the ruins of Tulum meant risking one's life. Even so, in 1896 Sylvanus G. Morley and J. L. Nusbaum did just this to become familiar with the site. In 1903 Tozzer tried to reach Tulum but was put off through fear of the Mayas.

Other expeditions reached Tulum between 1910 and 1914 and the Carnegie Institution, headed by S.G. Morley and S. Lothrop did important work between 1916 and 1922. Since 1938, the National Institute of Anthropology and History has been in charge of research on and conservation of the site.

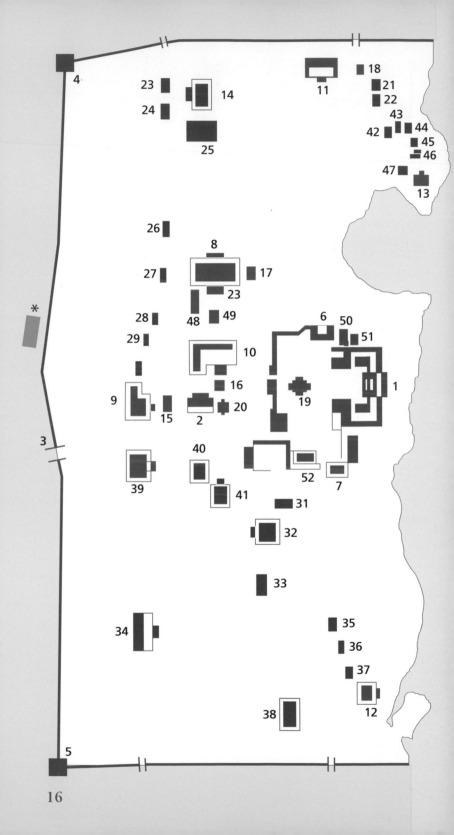

Map of Tulum

CARIBBEAN
SEA

The castle, 1

Temple of the Frescoes, 2

Entrance to the Wall, 3

Watchtower, 4 and 5

Temple of the Descending God, 6

Temple of the Initial Series, 7

House of the Halach Uinic, 8

House of the Chultún, 9

House of the Columns, 10

House of the Cenote, 11

Temple of the Sea, 12

Temple of the Wind, 13

House of the Northwest, 14

Shrines, 15, 16, 17 and 18

Ceremonial Platforms, 19 and 20

Dwelling Platforms 21, 22, 23, 24, 25, 26, 27, 28, 29, 30, 31, 32, 33, 34, 35, 36, 37 and 38

Tombs, 39, 40 and 41

Differents temples, shrines and platforms, 42, 43, 44, 45, 46, 47, 48, 49, 50, 51 and 52

* Bookshop

▼ Spectacular aerial view of Tulum showing the cliffs on which the ancient city stands, the small beach and the walled precinct.

The Great Wall

Five openings give access to the great ceremonial center: two in the north, two in the south and one in the west; the latter was perhaps the main one. All are narrow passages covered with vaults. The northeast entrance has the unusual feature of housing two small rooms near the inside passage of the wall. At present, access is in the north side and this allows one of the original entrances to be seen, which stands out because of its covering with the typical Maya vault or false arch.

Tulum is surrounded on three sides (north, south and west) by a wall of solid stone measuring 380 meters north-south by 170 meters east-west, with a thickness of 6 m., and a height of 4 m. The east side is open to the sea, since the high cliffs served as natural defense. Most of the monumental buildings of Tulum are located just within the walled precinct. It should be mentioned that the east ends of the wall do not reach the edge of the cliff face, but there are open spaces, which has led to the conjecture that the wall served to restrict access to the ceremonial and ritual area rather than function as military protection. In addition, the wall is not straight on all its path, but shows certain undulations, therefore it could represent the body of an enormous serpent which protected the symbolic sense of the precinct.

Watchtower

On the northeast and southwest sides of the wall stand structures that are reached by staircases resting against the interior wall. They are assumed to have functioned as watchtowers, an idea originally put forward by J. L. Stephens, who named them "Guard Houses," but, according to their characteristics, they must rather be considered temples. The ground plan of both buildings is very simple, rectangular in shape, with entrances in the south, east and west faces, while the inside holds a small altar resting against the north wall. One reason for rejecting a military function is that the southwest building has no opening to permit watching the western stretch of the wall. The decoration of the northwest (structure 55 or "House of the Aluxes") consists of a double molding outlining a smooth frieze which was painted blue. The crown is decorated with stepped borders, elements associated with the movement of the waters and the sky. On the southwest side of the building, between the moldings, there used to be also a small stucco figure of a descending god. All the façade used to be covered with outlined frescoes on a black background, but only a few fragments survive.

House of the Cenote

This stands in the northeast section of the precinct and has this name because it is located on an ancient cavity where water accumulates in the rainy season.

The building saw two stages of construction: it was first a square structure with two rooms, and later a small chamber was added in the southwest corner with an entrance in the south that was reached by a staircase.

In the east it has a portico of columns and inside there is a bench and a shrine. Under the floor of this building there is a tomb and an ossuary which contains the remains of several individuals. This is why the archaeologist Ernesto Vargas has suggested that this building could be an *Ajaw Naj*, "House of the Lords", where the remains of ruling lords were deposited.

House of the Northwest

This structure marks the northern end of what was the main street of Tulum and stands very near the northwest entrance of the wall. It has a rectangular floor plan and its main façade faces west and has a portico of two columns that form three entrances, reached by a staircase flanked by ramps.

The decoration is very sober: two lower moldings and one upper that frame the plain frieze. Inside are two rooms: the front one does not have anything special, but the rear one has a small shrine, a scale model of the temples. Next to this shrine is a narrow doorway that leads to a projection of the platform where there is a staircase into the plaza. This structure is not a temple but a palace-like building for residence by important people; no doubt the shrine was reserved for family worship, which was particularly important to the Mayas, since the divinization of ancestors was a custom. This habit seems influenced by Mayapán, in whose palaces there were shrines that stored pottery urns containing the ashes of the divinized ancestors. During the post-Classic, cremation was an important funerary practice.

▶Temple of the Wind

It projects on a natural rise of the cliff north of the archaeological site. It is a building with a single chamber with an entrance in the north; inside there are the remains of an altar and on the roof, remains of sculptures in very poor condition. The temple rises from a circular platform reached by steps. It is the only structure with a circular ground plan in Tulum and, by analogy with central Mexico it has been associated with the god of Wind *Ehécatl-Quetzalcóatl*, since the absence of corners favors the free circulation of the air. Similar buildings in the region have been found at Xcaret, Paamul and San Gervasio.

▼Shrines

Numerous structures identified as shrines or miniature temples have been recognized at Tulum. Some are very well preserved, while of others only the foundations remain. This type of construction is common on the east coast and is found in ceremonial precincts, near cenotes, caves, dwelling complexes and even on locations far from the coast. They functioned as sacred sites for the performance of rituals and offering ceremonies. Many are scale replicas of the large temples, with small chambers that sometime hold altars. Near the House of the Cenote, on a promontory facing the sea, there is a group of shrines; there is another group opposite the Temple of the Wind and three more in the center of the city.

House of the Halach Uinic

Halach Uinic means "Real Man" and is one of the terms the Mayas used to designate kings. It has received this name because of the dimensions of the building, as it is a palatial rectangular structure of enormous proportions. It stands on a platform which today has one access staircase, but it had four in earlier phases, later covered by remodeling, some leveling and the construction of an abutment. The main façade of the building has a portico with six bays formed by four columns and a pilaster; inside there are three rooms set in the north, south and east, with a shrine in the first one and three benches in the second. The whole group used to be covered by a large flat roof which has disappeared.

It is very possible that the façade was originally profusely decorated with stucco sculptures, to judge from the one that remains over the central inner doorway that connects the gallery with the shrine. This is an elaborate representation of the Descending God, a deity characteristic of the site. The structure still preserves traces of red and blue paint.

It is probable that this deity had special relevance on the site, and representations of him have been discovered even at Cobá and Ichpatuun near Chetumal. The figure has wings, wears an elaborate headdress and appears in a descending position, with the head downward and the legs bent upward. The exact identity of the personage is not known, although some historians have related him to a divinized lord, the setting Sun, an avocation of Venus, a swallow god or a bee god, since the region was an important producer of honey and wax.

► House of the Columns

This is also known as the "Great Palace" because it is the largest residential complex in the ancient city of Tulum. It stands on a large platform of one tier; it has an L-shaped ground plan, but the west wing was a later addition. The main façade, which faces south, has a wide portico of four columns: an additional gallery of columns served to support the gigantic flat roof. The inner room holds a shrine whose rear wall projects out of the panel of the north façade. The precinct has "curtain holders," that is to say small hollows in the walls with rings to secure curtains; it also has ventilation slits, the interiors decorated with crossed bars in the shape of an "X". The west wing of the building has a staircase and its own entrance portico. The building dates from the year 1075.

▼Dwelling platforms and tombs

The platforms are located in various sectors of the ancient settlement, mainly along the western edge of the street that crosses the precinct from south to north. Although they vary in size, all are very similar: they are low structures with one tier, almost always reached by staircases.

On several platforms, tombs have been discovered, consisting of large crypts covered with stone, roofed with slabs or vaults. The most important are those of structure 13, standing southwest of the inner precinct, a low platform reached by two small staircases.

Temple of the Frescoes

Both for its particular architecture and for its decoration and paintings that cover its walls, this structure is considered as having a vital social and religious function in the ancient settlement. It stands more or less in the center of the site, east of the main avenue and its building sequence reveals different stages. At first, it was a building with one level, a single roofed room with a Maya vault, with an entrance in the west and a small altar at the rear. Later, a gallery of columns was erected around the north, west and south sides of the original building, which became a shrine. A third phase included the construction of a new temple on top of the inner group; it has walls that show a strong outward slant, a chamber with an altar, reached by a staircase that existed at the south end; to strengthen the structure, the Mayas had to fill in part of the corridor of the first level and add buttresses and containing walls.

Opposite the Temple of the Frescoes is a small altar on which an interesting stela was carved, found next to the shrine and broken into three pieces. Although it has an inscription, erosion has prevented an adequate reading, but an allusion to the *katún 2 Ajaw* has been identified, which appears to commemorate the end of a Maya 20 year period. This monument appears to have been brought from Tankah.

Mural of the Temple of the Frescoes

The painting that used to decorate the precinct completely survives on the walls of the oldest temple of this monument. The predominant colors are Maya blue, gray, white and black, and the motifs are representations of different deities, such as *Chaac*, god of Rain, *Ix Chel*, goddess of the Moon, medicine, birth and weaving. There are also serpents that intertwine, scenes of offerings with abundant flowers, fruit and ears of corn, no doubt some related to fertility cults and rich harvests There are also rosettes and interlaced designs like knots associated with the symbol Pop, related to mats and therefore royal power.

▲ Façade of the Temple of the Frescoes

The main, west, front of the Temple of the Frescoes has moldings decorated with rosettes, human figures and interlaced volutes, which surround a frieze in which there are three niches, the lateral ones with representations of seated human figures who sport superb headdresses, while the central one is reserved for the famous Descending God. Between the moldings and the niches are bas-reliefs in stucco that show a man wrapped in a sort of interlaced rope. Over the entrance to the temple crowning the complex there is also a niche which was decorated with an image of the Descending God.

▲ Corner of the Temple of the Frescoes

On the southwest and northwest corners of the façade of the Temple of the Frescoes, over the friezes, there are enormous stucco masks that represent an old god, with decoration round the lower eyelid, a curved nose, prominent chin, turned down corners to his mouth and fangs. Originally they were painted orange, red and black. To judge by the attributes, this could be *Itzamná*, creator god and lord of the hierarchs, of the reigning Maya dynasties, also associated with the dew or substance from the sky, and consequently with rain, fertility and life.

House of the Chultún

This stands on a platform with staircases on the east and north sides, opposite the Temple of the Frescoes. Its name is due to the fact that it houses a chultún in the southwest corner of the platform, a bottle shaped underground deposit lined with stone slabs: it functioned as a cistern to store rainwater.

Like other palaces, it was probably the residence of some city official or dignitary. Its facade has an entrance portico formed of columns and the spacious inner precinct holds a shrine. At the north end another structure was added at some time, with two chambers that can be reached through a small doorway. An interesting fact is that a sight line can be drawn to the moldings on the Temple of the Descending god, the sunrise can be seen at the spring equinox, which is why it has an astronomical purpose. The entire building was covered with a flat roof of quarrystone held up by beams and timbers. The façade of the building collapsed 50 years ago, but above the main entrance there was a stucco sculpture of the head of a person. Likewise, over the doorway leading to the inner gallery there are the remains of the stone core of what was a sculpture of the Descending God. The inner walls were perhaps profusely decorated, since there are remains of black and red pigment.

The Tulum Cove and Maya trade

Between the inner precinct and the Temple of the Wind, the cliff is broken to form a small, pretty, easily reached beach of fine sand. The maneuvers of embarking and disembarking the canoes of the lords and merchants, are thought to have taken place here, since opposite the beach there is an esplanade with a platform that some authors associate with the market place of the ancient city.

An important economic activity of the Mayas was trade, which became especially relevant during the Late Post-Classic on the east coast. In geological explorations and also in historical sources, the development of an intense sea trade has been proved that linked the Gulf of Mexico with

the Gulf of Honduras and there is even evidence of products and objects from regions so distant as Costa Rica and Panama and central Mexico.

The Mayas created an intricate network of trade routes that linked various sites in the area and remote regions; this made the circulation of a wide variety pf products possible: salt, honey, wax, skins, precious feathers, tobacco, vanilla, rubber, shells, flint, obsidian, jadeite, quartz, turquoise, amber, pottery, basalt "metates", fish and dried meat, etc.

The Mayas of the coat also developed a system of aid for navigation by providing facilities for embarking and disembarking places. The system included different markers placed along the coast to indicate sources of fresh water, the natural passes through reefs or the presence of populations. Many of the temples and shrines built on the coast, as well as their symbolic function for rituals were at the same time

references for sailors. In addition, there was a system of signals made with smoke and flags to help navigation.

Maya trade was controlled by the noble class, who transported products in large canoes which could measure up to 16 meters long and were propelled by large groups of slave rowers who once on land became bearers. Navigation was coastal, in other words they never went very far away from the coastal fringe: when it was possible, they sailed in the shelter of barrier reefs, although in many sectors of the coast they had to sail in the open sea. In lake areas, sailing was on calm waters. For this reason, two types of craft were developed, one with a high prow, used on the open sea, and another for sailing on lagoons, with a low prow.

Monuments inside the inner precinct

Inside the area protected by the wall there is a second walled precinct 50 meters long on its north-south axis by 30 meters wide. Apparently it was the religious center of the settlement, since in it were planned such important structures as the Temple of the Descending God, the Temple of the Initial Series and the Castle, which is no doubt the ,most important structure of the ancient settlement. Although the buildings in this enclosure are not sited in absolute symmetry, in any case thcy comprise a group of well balanced architectural volumes. It is a sacred area, restricted to the ruling dynasty.

The Castle

Twelve meters tall, the Castle rises as the highest and most spectacular structure of Tulum. Its main façade overlooks the east end of the inner precinct, while the east one rises almost vertically on the edge of the cliff, which makes it easily seen from the sea. In fact, it is possible that it is "the great tower" described by the chaplain of the fleet of Grijalva in 1518. It was christened by the explorer J.L.Stephens, since seen from a distance it looks like a castle.

The building was constructed in various stages and different epochs: in the first phase, it was a low platform with two stepped tiers with a staircase in the west that served as a foundation for a palace of ample proportions, with a portico of nine columns and three long parallel galleries, the first two separated by a row of columns and the rear one by a wall with three doorways.

Later, the central part of this structure was covered to raise an additional story on which a new temple was built; the original staircase was lengthened to reach the new level, although in the process of filling, a vaulted passage was left with a small enclosure that contains some frescoes and an inscription, a line of persons in very elaborate costumes and a celestial band from which hangs a series of deities; strikingly in the center is the figure of the feathered serpent, the god of Rain and a cayman.

Opposite the upper temple also a stone was placed that was perhaps used for performing sacrifices. In the last stage of construction two small shrines were placed against the sides of the staircase: both have a single room, stand on low plinths and had flat roofs held up by wooden beams resting on two stone columns with square capitals. On one of the columns of the south shrine there was a stucco sculpture of a head, but it was destroyed on 1922.

The rear face of the Castle has a large sloping buttress which springs from a point very near the edge of the cliff, which affords a magnificent panoramic view from the sea. At both sides of the buttress there are two small windows that perhaps served the function of a lighthouse, since on stormy days, a light placed in each one of them served as a marker to indicate to sailors the "break" that is to say the natural passage through the reef.

Upper Temple of the Castle

The temple that crowns the Castle was planned during the second stage of construction: it has two vaulted rooms with benches inside. The façade has a portico with columns that form three entrances, and the columns are carved in the shape of serpents, with their heads formed by the bases and the rattles by the capitals, elements of the Maya-Toltec style like at Chichén Itzá that were introduced onto the Yucatán Peninsula by the enigmatic Itzáes; both on the columns and on the walls remains of the painting that decorated the precinct can be seen. The façade has three niches; the central one contains remains of the Descending God, while on the corners of the frieze are remains of masks.

Corner of the Temple of the Castle

On the corners of the main façade of this building, that is, the one that faces west, there were stucco masks located between the two cornices to form angles. They are masks with mouths open and teeth bared; they have large stylized eyes and wear elaborate feather headdresses.

Temple of the Initial Series

This is located at the southeast end of the inner precinct; it is a building with a single gallery, whose façade faces north and has one simple entrance. Its façade is very sober, since it has only one low double molding and one above that outlines the plain frieze, although over the entrance can be seen the remains of a stucco figure that no longer exists. The inner precinct has a vaulted ceiling, an altar and three doorways

The traveler J.L. Stephens had mentioned that in this building there were the remains of a stela. On undertaking the job of looking for it in 1911 the archaeologist Howe, found it divided in two segments under the supporting platform of the building. After a tortuous history, the stela was finally taken to the British Museum, perhaps by the explorer Thomas Gann, where it is housed at present. The important thing about this monument is that it has an interesting inscription with the initial series 9.6.10.0.0., in other words 564 A.D., a date much earlier than the occupation of Tulum by the Mayas from Tankáh at the time of founding the new city of Tulum. The discovery of this stela gave the name to the building.

Temple of the Descending God

This stands at the northeast end of the inner precinct and is thus known for the excellent sculpture that crowns the entrance. The platform that forms the base was at one time inside a building with a flat roof and a single room, which was filled in later to support the weight of the new construction. Also, a staircase was built leaning against the west side of the building, which is special because it has an orientation different from the upper temple.

The temple consists of one room with an entrance in the west and a Maya vault. At the rear of the enclosure there are two lateral benches and a narrow air inlet.

Both the main façade and the northwest and southwest corners and the interior of the temple were profusely decorated.

Over the entrance to the temple there is a sculpture of a winged god with the head down, arms hanging and legs bent upward in a descending position, as if the figure were descending from the sky; this gives the name Descending God.

On several buildings of the ancient city, similar figures can be seen; this has led some scholars to think the site was a special center of worship for the god, considered a regional god of the coast, associated according to some researchers with Venus and the rain, the evening star, the setting Sun, a swallow god and even a god of bees, since the production of honey was extremely important in the region.

The archaeologist S. Iwaniszewski discovered that the building records the phenomenon of the winter solstice: shortly after sunrise, the light penetrates the window of the east wall and lights up the lower part of the façade, below the hands of the deity.

Shrines facing the Caribbean Sea

At a short distance northwest of the Temple of the Wind stands a group of three small shrines. The ground plan of the three is very simple: a single vaulted room with one entrance. Two of the shrines are oriented to the south and one to the east. The south wall of one of them is partially built with carved fragments of what appears to be a broken stela. Facing these structures there were some elements, for example two stakes to hold stucco sculptures, a column and the remains of a "pineapple," which is a stucco sculpture perhaps associated with the sacred ceiba tree.

Just at the foot of the stairs of the Temple of the Wind there are two other altars and a shrine, also associated with other small altars and stucco elements. One of the altars is rectangular, but there is no staircase, with a sort of circular chimney at the top, perhaps for burning incense. The shrine is larger than the others and has four entrances at the cardinal points.

Temple of the Sea

This stands at the southeast end of the site and is a temple typical of the east coast style whose façade is oriented toward the sea. It has a single room with one entrance, and inside is a small altar. Its roof, now lost, was flat and held up by wooden beams. During the visit of J.L.Stephens, the roof was perfectly well preserved. The explorer even mentions that the four main wooden beams were in good condition and held up a series of wooden trusses that supported the quarry-stone of the roof. The façade of the building is very sober: two low moldings and one high one that surround a smooth frieze, although in earlier times everything must have been covered with stucco and perhaps decorated extensively with paintings, like other temples. It is interesting that this building looks over the sea, probably in connection with some special cult to the rising sun, the sea or even trade. The building stands on a low platform with a narrow staircase in front.

Temple of the Nauyaca

The different buildings that are located inside the walled precinct of Tulum do not represent the whole of the archaeological site. The remains of the ancient settlement stretch for more than six kilometers along the coast. Around the walled precinct there are numerous dwelling complexes consisting of platforms, altars, caves and cenotes: in fact, there is a second wall that protects a vast extent of the ancient population center. An example of the latter are the temples located south of the walled precinct in the zone of huts and camps, as well as the fine temple of the "Nauyaca," a building crowned by a triangular crest standing on the crags of the coast one kilometer and a half from the wall.

> ▶ "We traveled this coast a day and a night, and the next day, when the sun was about to set we saw in the far distance a town or village so large that the city of Seville could not appear larger or better and a very big tower could be seen".

> Juan Díaz. May 7, 1518

Printed in:
Stellar Group, S.A. de C.V.
E. Rebsamen 314 y 315, Narvarte
03020, México D.F.
5639-2342 / 5639-1850
May, 2006